UNDERSTANDING
ECOLOGY

UNDERSTANDING
ECOLOGY

ELIZABETH T. BILLINGTON

Illustrations by Robert Galster

Frederick Warne and Co., Inc.   New York and London

ACKNOWLEDGEMENTS

The author wishes to express her appreciation for the help and encouragement given by Sheldon Levine, Science Consultant for the Elementary Schools, Mamaroneck, N.Y. and M. Carlton Van Patten, Professor of Biology, Westchester Community College, Valhalla, N.Y., both of whom read the manuscript.

For Feller,
A GOOD COMPANION WHOSE NICHE
HAS NOT BEEN FILLED.

CONTENTS

UNDERSTANDING ECOLOGY

INTRODUCTION

Ecology (ee-kol-o-je) is the study of the interchanging relationships of living things to each other and to their environment. This is a new and important science and its name is not well known. Nearly one hundred years ago a German biologist, Ernst Haeckel, first suggested ecology as a separate field of biology. He formed the word ecology by putting together two Greek words, 'oikos,' which means home or place to live and 'logos' which means science. Ecology, then is the 'home science,' the study of the place where man lives.

In 1900, the serious study of ecology as a science distinct from the other branches of biology began. Today, however, scientists and many others realize the great need for a more exact understanding of the relationships of *all* parts of the world of nature.

Early man needed to know the laws of nature in order to remain alive. He had to know which plants and berries he could safely eat and where they could be found. It was necessary for him to know where the water was pure, where and when he could catch the largest fish, where and when he could trap or hunt animals to provide the best food, clothing, bedding, fuel and bow strings. He had to know which people and animals were friendly. He had to understand the effect of weather and changing seasons on his food supply and need for shelter. Necessity forced early man to gain a knowledge of ecology.

The same laws of nature apply to modern man. As civilization has grown complex, man seems to have gained control of natural resources. It appears that he has set himself apart from the rest of the world of nature. As the human population of the world increased, man's relationship to the rest of the natural world changed. Yet he sometimes forgets that the laws of nature apply to him as well as to the rest of the natural world.

Modern man has to learn how to keep the air, water and soil free of harmful materials such as insecticides, waste and radioactive materials. He must learn how to keep soil from eroding and how to keep it fertile. By studying nature's population problems and how nature makes use of the sun's energy, man may find the answer to the great problem of feeding the increased human population.

This book will help you to explore the science of ecology and to understand what happens in the natural world. It will help you explore your natural home and enjoy finding, understanding and respecting the give-and-take among all living things.

If your interest is in insects, birds, animals, plants or rocks; you may discover how they fit into the total scheme of the natural world. This book was written not only for people who live in the country or suburban areas, but also for the city dweller—for he too is surrounded by the world of nature and subject to its laws.

To help you understand new scientific words, an index with reference glossary has been included. It shows the page on which the definition appears. The definition will be easy to find because the word will be printed in *italics*.

Chapter 1

GETTING READY TO EXPLORE

Before going exploring, you must get the equipment needed to carry on a search. Most important to an ecologist is curiosity—a desire to know, to be ready to ask why, how, when and where things happen. He must learn never to take anything for granted and not to jump hastily to conclusions.

The power to observe is also necessary. The ecologist must go slowly, be patient and take time to look at everything—to touch, smell and listen. He must keep accurate records of what he sees.

Here is a list of useful equipment:

1. A small magnifying glass marked '10X' which will magnify what you look at ten times. Through it you can see many details of plants, insects, fungi, rocks, bird feathers and many other things.

2. A small plastic ruler (bright in color, so that you don't lose it) to help you estimate the size of birds and accurately measure plants or rocks. It serves also as a good 'poker' and 'lifter' when you investigate anything from a rotting log to a tide pool.

3. A small notebook and a pencil for keeping an accurate record of where you went, what you saw and the conditions at the time.

4. A thermometer to help relate the effects of changes in temperature in the natural world.

5. Envelopes in which to keep specimens and on which to record where and when you found them.

6. Plastic containers to keep specimens for temporary observation.

A trained ecologist uses the knowledge discovered by many scientists—biologists, chemists, geologists, physicists and so on. After careful study, he puts the facts together to explain how parts of nature are related to one another. This makes it possible for an ecologist to look ahead, to see what will happen.

Try being an ecologist right now. Test your curiosity and power of observation by watching a tree. In your notebook, record everything you notice about the tree—even what lives in it or visits it.

If you live in a city and do not have a tree near enough to observe each week, keep a record of everything you notice happening on your window sill or fire escape.

Here are some things you might record and answer: the date, time of day, temperature and weather. Are there any birds? Why do they come, or why don't they come? Are there any insects? Is there any fungus, lichen or moss? Are there flowers on the tree or seeds of any sort?

This will start you on an interesting project, but you will need something more to help you explore ecology—an understanding of the words used by ecologists. The following chapters explain some of them.

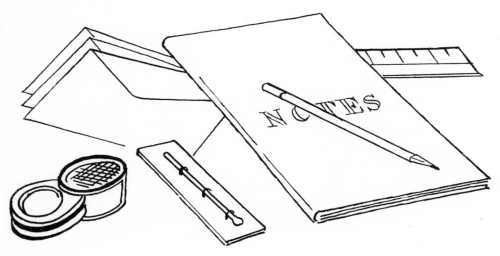

OBSERVATION OF A TREE

SPECIES: Norway Maple. Identified last summer when leaves were on the tree. I used "TREES" a Golden Nature Guide to verify identity.

PLACE: In front of Mr. Knight's house. Mr. Knight said it was planted about ten years ago to replace a diseased elm tree. He said the town Nature Council recommended Norway Maple which is not troubled by road dust.

TIME: January 10, 1968 — 4 P.M.

WEATHER: Sunny, cold, temperature 36° F

CONDITION: Tree trunk dry. No leaves. Buds show. No occupants, two blue-jays visited tree and gray squirrel ran up tree while I talked to Mr. Knight.

TIME: March 10, 1968 — 4PM

WEATHER: Clear and Sunny, temperature 40°

CONDITION: Snow piled about the tree trunk which looks wet. Buds don't look any different. — Sparrow was in tree.

TIME: April 10, 1968 — 4PM

WEATHER: Clear, sunny and much lighter than when I was observing tree at the same time in January — 55°

CONDITION: Tree trunk dry. Buds are bigger and can be seen easily. I notice little twigs like this. Mr. Knight said these twigs are left from last year's flowers after the seeds fell. A starling came and went from the tree.

Fritz Henle / PHOTO RESEARCHERS

Chapter 2

ENVIRONMENT

Look up from this page. Take a careful look all around you. What do you see? A room in your home? A school room? A library? The inside of a bus, train or car? Or are you out of doors? Wherever you are, all that you see is a part of what a scientist calls your environment (en-vi-ron-ment). Actually, it is much more than what you can see right now. *Environment* is the surroundings and influence in which any person or thing lives, grows or develops. It is made up of two groups: one of living things—plants and animals, and a second of non-living things such as rocks, air, sunlight and water.

Scientists once tried to make an orderly list of things which make up environment. But they found it confusing and tiresome so they stopped. However, out of it came the science of ecology when they tried to explain what they had found. They had found the non-living environment of earth, water, air and sunlight to be a complex system. They discovered that they could not separate the system from living things—plants and animals which depend for life on the non-living. In short, they discovered that all parts of the environment work together, giving to and receiving from each other the things necessary for life.

The sun's heat and energy, the smoke, dust, and pollen carried in the air, the soil, and the water that falls as rain or snow all make up part of your environment. These determine the kinds of plants and trees which share your environment. These plants, in turn, determine the kinds of birds and animals which will share it.

Things you cannot see are also an important part of your environment. The warmth and dryness of your home helps to keep you well. Love shared by a family creates happiness and peace of mind and aids in its survival.

Think about this. When you are indoors, the building you are in is not just *your* environment. It is also the environment of other forms of life which share it with you. Many plants and animals take advantage of "your" shelter, food and water. They make homes and raise families. In doing this, these other forms of life are not only taking food and shelter, they are also helping to create and change your environment.

You may have said, "I have no animals in my home or school." Stop and think. If you look closely you will find many forms of life— a mouse, a cockroach, a spider, a moth, a cricket or birds nesting under the eaves.

It may be hard to believe that the small house-mouse sharing your shelter and food may affect you. He may, however; but not because of the amount of food he takes. He can carry disease germs. Mice may be attacked by fleas which in turn may carry and transfer the deadly bubonic plague to humans.

All of man's efforts to force the cockroach to stop sharing his home have failed. This amazing insect has slowly spread around the world, following man. He feeds on crumbs which man drops or the food he leaves. He spoils the food and leaves an odd, unpleasant odor.

Spiders spinning their silk webs change your environment when they eat thousands of harmful insects each year.

The clothes moth secretly shares your environment living on woolen blankets, sweaters, scarves and gloves. The holes he makes certainly affect all of us.

Chirruping house crickets may add a happy song to your home but they also bite holes in damp clothes to get water.

These creatures are sharing and creating your environment. They help make your environment a busy place. Much is going on all of the time and changes take place constantly in your environment.

The best way to explore your environment is bit by bit, a little at a time. In this way you may look more closely and carefully, then you will understand better how all things in nature depend on each other, and how they work together.

Chapter 3

ECOSYSTEMS

Ecologists use the term *ecosystem* (ee-ko-system) to describe any area in which you will find living organisms and non-living things working together, exchanging the materials of life and using them over and over again. The exchange of materials never ends. It is necessary for life to go on.

Every ecosystem has four parts. Some people say this part of ecology can be thought of as the "who-eats-whom-and-why" part.

The first part of any ecosystem is made up of the non-living substances or, to be more scientific, inorganic substances of the environment. These include water, carbon dioxide, nitrogen, phosphorous, air and minerals. These are among the necessities of an ecosystem and help plants to grow and replace natural waste. A small part of these is ready to be used right away. Some is held for future use. How fast or slowly inorganic substances are released is important, because they are food and so regulate the rate of work of the entire ecosystem.

The second part of an ecosystem is its living substances or organisms, some of which are called "producers" or food makers. In all the world of nature, only green plants are able to make energy-filled food. This process, called *photosynthesis* (foh-to-sin-the-sis), is the means by which green plants, exposed to the light of the sun, combine carbon dioxide and water to produce basic food substances.

An ecosystem's third part consists of the living organisms—mostly animals—which are called the "consumers," because they feed on the green plants. These consumers, however, also serve as food for other consumers. The animals which eat green plants but not other animals are called *herbivores* (her-be-vors). They are also called *primary consumers* or first eaters, because their food is the sugar and other food substances stored in green plants. A few herbivores are rabbits, cows, sheep, porcupine and chipmunks.

The animals that feed on herbivores are called *carnivores* (kahr-ne-vors), which means flesh-eaters. Many carnivores also eat green plants or fruits as well as meat. *Secondary consumers* is another name given to carnivores because they feed on herbivores or first consumers. Some carnivores are foxes, dogs, cats, hawks, and of course, you.

The very important fourth part of any ecosystem is the *decomposers* —the organisms which break down tissues and excretions of other organisms to simpler forms. Most of the decomposers are bacteria and fungi. Bacteria do most of their work in breaking down dead animal flesh. Fungi, such as mushrooms, generally work at breaking down plant material. Both are important and must work together so that the chemical substances return to the ecosystem to be used again.

Many people think it unpleasant to speak of bacteria and fungi eating dead things. However, if they did not do this, life could not continue. Imagine what it would be like if every dead tree lay where it had fallen. What if all the remains of ancient animals were piled up everywhere and not changed? There would be no room for new life. All the materials necessary for life would be locked up in dead plants and animal bodies. Fungi and bacteria rework the nutrients green plants have made and put them to their own use. In doing this, they release important substances into the soil.

A pond is an ecosystem. You could not possibly investigate all of the processes in a pond ecosystem. However, you can see how closely related and dependent each part is on all the other parts. Try making an observation of a pond if you live near one. Here are a few questions to answer:

Is it a natural pond or was it made by man? Where does the water come from? Where does it go? What kind of animals live in the pond and on its banks? Who visits the pond? At what time? Why do they visit? What kind of plants live in the pond? What are their names? Do you see any insects near the pond or on the water? What are they?

SIMPLE POND ECOSYSTEM

PART 1 Organic and inorganic substances such as oxygen, calcium, phosphorus salts, etc. A small part of these nutrients are ready to be used right away. A larger part is held back especially in the sediments at the bottom of the pond.

PART 2
PRODUCERS
A. Tiny floating plants, usually algae, which live all through the pond as far down as the sunlight reaches. They are the food factory of the pond.

B. Plants rooted in shallow water or large floating plants which provide food and shelter for many different animals.

PART 3
CONSUMERS
A. Primary consumers—Herbivores who feed directly on the green plants or algae.

B. Secondary consumers — Carnivores who feed on the primary consumers.

PART 4
DECOMPOSERS
Water bacteria and fungi which are found all through the pond but especially in the mud-water on the bottom. They feed on dead plants, animals or their feces. They help release chemical substances so they may be reused in the cycle of life.

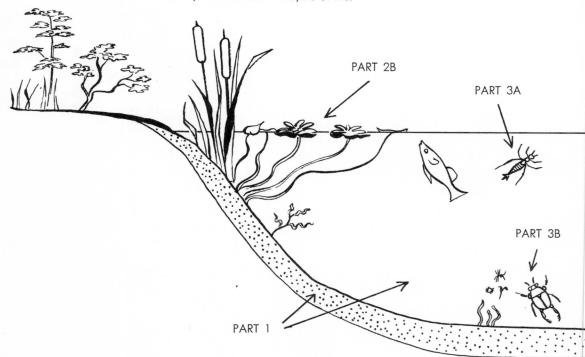

PART 2B

PART 3A

PART 3B

PART 1

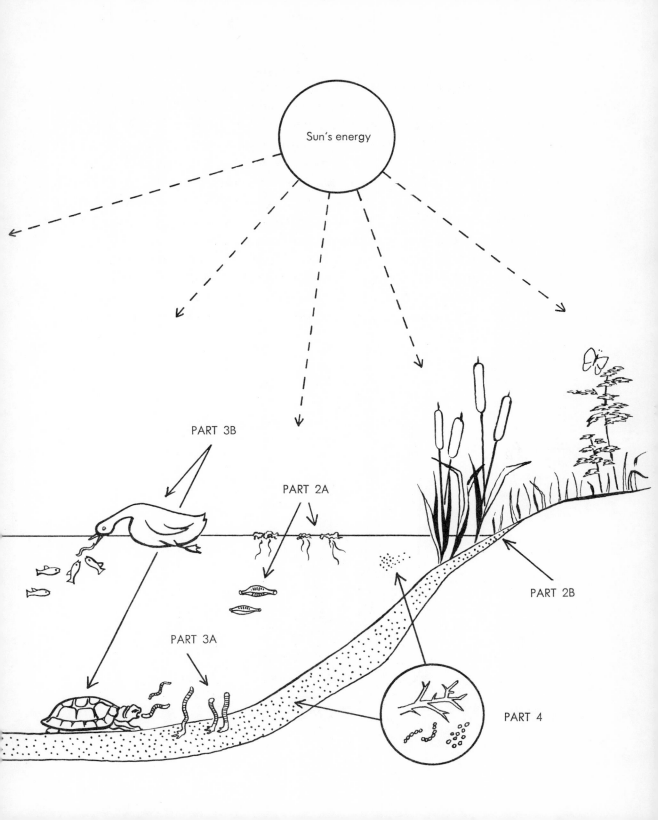

Sun's energy

PART 3B

PART 2A

PART 3A

PART 2B

PART 4

You will find a library book on pond life a great help. If you do not live near a pond, you can make a simple aquarium at home and see a working ecosystem. Use a plain gallon jar with a wide mouth, a plastic vegetable crisper, or a tank with a metal frame and slate bottom made just for this purpose. Whatever you use, be sure it is clean. Wash it carefully with clear water before you place in it about one and a half inches of sandy soil. Press about four water plants firmly into the sand. You can buy these at a pet shop. If you have questions, the people at the petshop can help you.

On the sand, place a flat rock. Carefully pour the water on the rock so the sand and plants will not be disturbed. Fill the container to about two inches from the top. Let the aquarium alone for about a week. The plants need time to put out roots before you put in the animals.

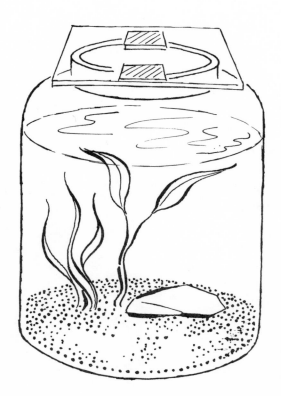

Place the container where there is good light but little direct sunlight. Direct sun would warm the water and make the algae and green plants grow too fast.

The size of the container determines how many snails and fish you need for proper balance in your ecosystem. "One inch of fish to a gallon of water" is a good rule to follow. When you measure a fish under this rule do not include its tail. You can keep a snail and two fish not more than one inch long in a gallon jar. Experiment and find out.

Dust and dirt will enter the container unless you cover it with glass. Rest it on thin pieces of cork so that fresh air can circulate in the space over the water.

Perhaps, as a beginning ecologist, you want to watch and record just one part of the ecosystem. If the decomposers interest you, make a record of the various places where you see fungi at work in your neighborhood. Some will be high above the ground on trees. Some will be found only if you keep your eyes on the ground. You may find a puff ball or a mushroom in a meadow or near a fire hydrant. You may watch some fungi at work in your kitchen. Bread mildew is a fungus working to decompose the bread.

If you want to watch a fungus grow and work, scrape a little of the vein of blue cheese onto a piece of rye bread. Add just a few drops of milk and place the bread in a dark place for about ten days. In that time, the fungus will cover the bread. With a magnifying glass, you can watch its growth.

You can also observe fungus growing on fruits and see how the temperature affects it. Keep a record of the different rates of growth of fungus on fruit stored at room temperature, in a refrigerator and in a freezer compartment.

Chapter 4

BALANCE OF NATURE

When you find out how an ecosystem works, you realize that the work of nature is not just a mixed up jumble of living things that happen to be in a certain place. There is a definite order. The air, the water, the soil, plants and animals all work, contributing to the whole ecosystem. When people speak of the *balance of nature,* they are talking about the tendency of living things to keep a balance among themselves and with their environment.

By observing an ecosystem, you learn about the balance of nature. You already know that you cannot put two gallons of water into a one-gallon jar. The water would spill over. The jar will hold one gallon of water and no more; this is called its carrying capacity. An ecosystem too has a *carrying capacity;* it is the number of each kind of animal or plant which the ecosystem can supply with enough water, food and living space. If you put too many plants or fishes in a one-gallon jar, there will not be enough water, food and space for all. Some will die. This is also true in natural ecosystems.

Let us suppose that in a certain place the deer population increased greatly and there was not enough shelter, water or food for all. What would happen to the extra deer? They would be removed in several different ways. Some might die of disease, others serve as easier prey for carnivores. The lack of shelter might cause some deer to die from exposure to bad weather. A few would leave the area to find a better place to make their homes. The healthy deer would remain and adapt to the carrying capacity of the land, and the balance would be restored.

Studies of ecosystems show that unless something extreme—such as fire, earthquake, or flood—happens, a balance is usually kept fairly well for a long time. But, when a balance is upset or destroyed, a new balance must slowly be worked out. It is done by animals and plants adjusting to the carrying capacity of the land.

In order to survive, every living thing must have water, air, energy from the sun, and minerals from the soil. The supply of these helps create environment and affects the carrying capacity of an ecosystem.

If water, food or any other necessity of life is scarce, the number of plants and animals found in a given area becomes smaller. Only life able to adapt to the shortage can survive. This is called the *limiting factor,* and means the supply of the physical materials necessary for life which is in limited supply.

Temperature may be a limiting factor. The polar bear with his heavy insulating fur and fat has adapted for living in cold climates. His life is limited by temperature to places where it averages no more than 32° F.

To desert plants and animals, the limiting factor is the amount of water available. To the plants of the shady woodland floor, it is the amount of sunlight able to filter through the leaves overhead.

Not enough rainfall can be a limiting factor in any ecosystem. In a dry year, fewer plants grow in an ordinarily thick meadow. Then the meadow mice have less to eat. They reproduce in smaller numbers and the fox who hunts them for food goes hungry. The fox may catch some rabbits or find berries to eat, but he too will reproduce fewer offspring. Too much rainfall can also be a limiting factor. In a wet year, heavy rains can cause a brook or pond to flood. Nearby plants, insects and animals would be affected.

Limiting factors are interesting balances of nature because they may be caused in so many different ways. They, in turn, reach out within their environment to affect everything else living there.

Man is the most powerful being in any ecosystem because of his ability to change its operation. His ability seems to grow faster than his understanding of the results of the changes he makes. If a man should make too many errors in changing ecosystems, he could upset the delicate balance beyond the point where it can recover. This is a real and great danger. Man has a practical as well as a moral responsibility to keep the ecosystem in good working order. Scientists know that the careless use of water, air and soil is dangerous. Man must learn to keep ecosystems in balance and allow nature constantly to renew our means of life.

Keeping the balance of nature is a great new adventure about which ecologists are finding out more each day. Maybe you will become one of them.

Chapter 5

THE BIOSPHERE

Do you realize that you live in the most complete ecosystem of all—the *biosphere?* It is a thin layer about the earth where it is possible for life to be carried on. The biosphere reaches as far below the earth's surface as the longest root is able to push. It stretches as far above the earth as the tallest tree and as far as the wind is able to carry pollen, spores and seeds. The biosphere includes salt water and fresh water to the depth that life is carried on in them. In the biosphere, the incoming rays of the sun work, making essential physical and chemical changes in lifeless material.

Birds may fly high into the sky and leave the biosphere, but they must return if they are to go on living. In recent years man has learned to leave the biosphere for a short time only because he has found ways to take along air, water and food.

The biosphere seems to be filled with invisible "fences" which keep plants and animals in certain places. These fences are heat, cold, dampness, dryness, or the wrong kind of food or soil. Man has the ability to cross the fences and to adapt to various parts of the biosphere. He makes his home anywhere.

In his great migrations, man looked for places where he found weather and soil like those of his homeland. He had good reason for doing this as he knew from experience how to work a certain kind of soil and what crops he could grow well in it.

When explorers of long ago travelled the globe, they marvelled at the strange and colorful birds, animals and plants they found. Often they would bring back the surprising creatures and plants from other parts of the world. Most people who saw them for the first time

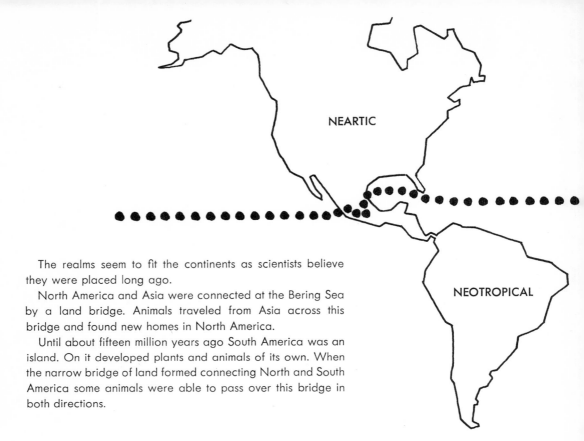

NEARTIC

NEOTROPICAL

The realms seem to fit the continents as scientists believe they were placed long ago.

North America and Asia were connected at the Bering Sea by a land bridge. Animals traveled from Asia across this bridge and found new homes in North America.

Until about fifteen million years ago South America was an island. On it developed plants and animals of its own. When the narrow bridge of land formed connecting North and South America some animals were able to pass over this bridge in both directions.

wondered about them, but no one tried to find out why they were so different. However, in 1858, Philip L. Sclater gathered together information about them. He listed them according to where each had come from.

In 1876, another naturalist with an inquiring mind, Alfred Russel Wallace, who was interested in all of nature, studied Sclater's work. He reviewed the listings carefully and after making a few changes, he came to the conclusion that the world could be divided into six land areas or, as he called them, *zoogeographic* (zoh-o-je-og-ra-fic) realms. Today scientists still recognize these realms. Study of these realms

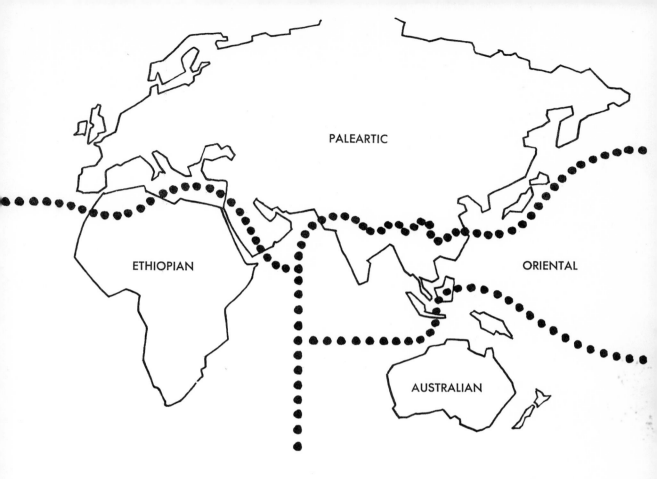

shows that each has separate forms of life which are found nowhere else. Each realm is separated from the others by impassable boundaries of climate, water or mountains. Because similar conditions are found in different places on earth, similar species of animals and plants have developed in them. There are reindeer in the European tundra and related caribou in the Canadian tundra. In the grasslands of North America there are coyotes and ground squirrels, and in the grasslands of Africa there are lions and zebras. Each species carries on the same work in keeping the balance of nature. Because of this, ecologists call them replacement species.

31

Chapter 6

BIOMES

Scientists find it useful to divide the biosphere into biomes. A *biome* is a large geographic area with a somewhat uniform climate. The length of the seasons is similar in all parts of each biome and, of course, so is the length of days. Over a long period, the climate has made the conditions good for certain plants to adapt to living there. These plants dominate the biome and usually a biome gets its name from the dominant plant. The plants, in adapting to the climate, have in turn created a special kind of environment in which only certain kinds of birds, animals and insects can gather food, find shelter and raise young.

THE DECIDUOUS (de-sid-yew-us) FOREST BIOME

Here summers are warm and winters are cold. As the seasons slowly change, the lengths of day and night change also. There is enough rainfall for deciduous trees to grow and develop. The name, deciduous, comes from the Latin word which means "to fall off," as the leaves of some trees do in autumn. As the days grow shorter and the weather turns colder, the trees cannot get enough water from the cold ground to replace the moisture they lose from the broad surfaces of their leaves. Strong winter winds speed the loss of moisture. The falling of the leaves slows the activity inside the tree. Then there is less need for water. In winter they may be surrounded by snow while the frost in the ground cuts off their water supply.

Trees which thrive in this climate are beech, maple, hickory, oak and elm. Blue jays, hairy woodpeckers, chickadees, owls and hawks build nests, gather food and breed here. With the spring, different

32

Courtesy of the AMERICAN MUSEUM OF NATURAL HISTORY

birds come to build nests and raise young. They migrate to warmer climates and other feeding grounds in winter.

Other animals which find this forest a good place to make homes are woodchuck, chipmunk, squirrel, racoon, red fox, Virginia white-tailed deer and black bear. After a summer of raising young and gathering food, the woodchuck and chipmunk take shelter and hibernate during winter in the earth under the fallen leaves which form a deep and warm cover. In *hibernation* (hy-ber-nay-shon) an animal lies still, the temperature of its body drops, its heartbeat slows and it uses up body fat stored for use when no food can be found. It is like a tree's losing its leaves and slowing activity to the smallest amount possible. Hibernation allows an animal to remain alive even when no food is available.

In winter the bare forest also gives shelter and food to deer and the red fox. The force of the cold wind is cut by the leafless trees. The forest offers a more moderate climate than open spaces. The deer feed on twigs and tree bark. The hungry red fox seeks the busy squirrels who spend a lot of time on the forest floor hunting for nuts hidden so carefully during the warm summer.

Man finds this biome a good place to live. It is quite probable that early man lived for a long time at the edge of this kind of forest. Food was easily found in edible herbs and berries. Small animals, deer and birds came to find food, so man had game to eat. Man most likely first started to cultivate plants for food in the rich, crumbly, soft soil at the edge of the deciduous forest.

In this biome civilization developed to its highest point. And, of course, it is here that man has interfered most with the natural world. In fact, he has cleared so many trees and covered so much soil with cement and asphalt that parts of it can no longer be thought of as belonging to it.

CONIFEROUS (ko-nif-er-us) FOREST BIOME

In this biome, temperatures are low all year. The lengths of day and night vary greatly according to season. Summer's long days are cool and moist, and the winter is long and extremely cold. Winter days are short. The snowfall is heavy and may completely cover the smaller trees, forming a blanket which keeps warmth in and cold out.

All things here have to adapt to the cold and dryness of winter and

34

be able to carry on life in spite of it. The biome got its name from the cone-bearing trees, the conifers, which adapted to this difficult climate.

The spruce tree is probably the best known of the conifers which grow here. Of the animals, the moose is best known. He feeds on the spruce, enjoying the young twigs and leaves in summer and the bark in winter. Ecologists sometimes call it the "spruce-moose" biome. Other animals which live in the coniferous forest are the lynx, wolverine and porcupine. In winter, animals from the tundra, the biome discussed next, seek refuge in the northern edge of this biome.

Courtesy of the AMERICAN MUSEUM OF NATURAL HISTORY

Many birds migrate to these woodlands in summer when plenty of food is available. They return to the south when cold weather cuts off their supply of food. The red crossbill, however, has made a special adaptation and seldom leaves. His odd snipper beak is so formed that he can pick the seed from the cones. Now, to survive, he must live where cone-bearing trees are found.

The great grey owl, spruce grouse and the Canada jay find this forest a pleasant place to live.

The Coniferous Forest Biome is of great importance to man. For many centuries it has supplied him with lumber for building and valuable wood pulp for paper.

TUNDRA (tun-dra) BIOME

The Tundra Biome was given its name by the people of Lapland who were driven north when their homeland was invaded long ago. In order to remain alive, they had to adapt to the new and difficult climate and live close to the great herds of reindeer found there. Laplanders still live closely with their reindeer herds, following them north as the reindeer feed on the tundra in the short summer and south to the northern limits of the coniferous forest in winter.

This cold and windy biome is found between the northern parts of the coniferous forest and the permanent ice and snow of the north polar cap. Winter lasts for nine cold, dark months of little daylight. A three-month summer of short nights and nearly constant daylight is the other season. Even during summer, the subsoil of the tundra does not thaw. Lichen, mosses and a few sheltered but stunted trees live here. In winter this biome seems a waste, but during the almost continuous daylight of summer, plants burst from the ground. The flowers mature and develop seed quickly before the short summer ends. Great flocks of water fowl, swans and Canada geese spend the summer nesting and fly to warmer climates for the winter. The ptarmigan is the only land bird which makes its home here all the year around.

The arctic fox, musk oxen and a few wolves share the cold windy weather of tundra winter. It is far too cold in winter for animals to hibernate. Animals that do stay through the winter have adapted by growing heavy coats of fur. Their bodies are rugged and compact like that of the musk ox.

Man has studied the weather here, and he has not found it a good place to live.

Courtesy of the AMERICAN MUSEUM OF NATURAL HISTORY

GRASSLANDS BIOME

The Grasslands Biome is usually found in a continent's center. Its name comes from the main plant life found there—grass. The summer is usually quite warm. The rainfall does not provide enough water for trees to grow, but there is enough moisture to keep a desert from forming.

The grasses are of different heights—according to the amount of rain. Some of the tallest grasses grow to six feet in height. The grass roots grow the same distance into the rich soil and hold it firmly in place. Over many years the grasses have built deep layers of rich topsoil because the leaves die at the end of each season and quickly decay, returning to soil.

Courtesy of the AMERICAN MUSEUM OF NATURAL HISTORY

The animals that originally made the grasslands their home adapted to the area. They learned to burrow in the soft earth or to run swiftly to escape predators. For additional protection, they live in colonies or herds. The American bison was an important animal of the grasslands of central North America. This animal was nearly wiped out by white men who killed millions of them. The first migrating white men wished to use the grasslands for pasture for sheep and cattle. And today man has replaced the animals, and most of the great seas of wild grass are now fields of wheat, corn and barley.

Ground squirrels, prairie dogs, coyotes, jack rabbits, prairie falcons, prairie chickens and meadow larks can still be found in the grasslands. Only in protected areas can bison still be found.

Man has abused this biome which produces much of his food. Many farms have been abandoned because of crop failure due to drought. Soil erosion and over use of the soil caused crop failure because man has not paid attention to ecological laws. He did not find out which crops the climate and the soil could best produce. Today, he is learning to rotate crops to enrich the soil and to prevent animals from over-grazing.

DESERT BIOME

The climate of the Desert Biome is severe. The desert is not always hot and dry. It is extremely hot during the day when the temperature may go to over 100° F. At night the temperature can fall rapidly to near freezing. Plants and animals have always adapted to great changes in order to survive anywhere.

Desert plants do not grow close to each other so that their long roots can spread out close to the top of the soil and gather any rain water which falls. This leaves much bare soil exposed to water and wind. In most deserts there is occasional rain which washes away soil because the plants are not close enough together to hold it in place. The roots of the plants do not reach deep enough to act as a

sponge and hold water. The run-off of water is rapid; in fact, it flows faster than a man can run. In a sudden flash flood, a man may drown in the desert as the water speeds along carrying with it soil, boulders and plants.

Wind is also a sand mover. Since there is no plant cover to act as a windbreak, the sand moves quickly for great distances. Desert plants and rocks are always being scoured by wind-blown sand. Plants are affected by both wind and water. Floods may uproot them and bury

40

or break them. The wind may strip their leaves or branches. Wind-driven sand may wear away their protective covering. To meet these trying conditions, desert plants grow little foliage and form thick skins to help them contain water and resist the wind. The cactus is probably the best known desert plant. Its stems and branches are fleshy. In place of leaves it grows spines.

Many people think of the desert as a lonesome and uninhabited place. This is because most desert animals are active only in the early morning or evening. At those times the desert temperature is moderate, and desert animals have not made so many adaptions to their difficult environment as the plants. This may be because they are able to move from place to place and escape some of the hardships of desert life.

Some desert animals are *nocturnal* (nok-tur-nal) and seek food and carry on their lives at night. They do not have to go out in the sun, but spend the hot day underground or in a shady refuge.

When the hot dry season comes to the desert, some animals *aestivate* (es-ti-vate), which means they pass the summer in a deep sleep as forest animals do when they hibernate. Usually desert animals are small like the desert mule deer, the horned lizard, peccary (wild hog), pack and kangaroo rat and native snakes. Birds of the desert are the elf owl, turkey vulture and cactus wren.

Man, too, has for centuries tried to make a life for himself in the desert. People who live in the Sahara Desert of North Africa wander from one place to another. They keep small herds of goats and sheep. Because rainfall is uneven, they travel to where rain has recently fallen and plants have grown. In the deserts of the old world, explorers find many ruins of irrigation systems. These show how man tried but failed to bring water to the desert and grow food.

Scientists today realize that an understanding of the laws of the ecosystem is necessary if they are to succeed in growing food in the desert.

41

TROPICAL FOREST BIOME

This biome lies in the tropics on either side of the equator. The temperature is hot and quite uniform all year around. It is just about as wet as it is hot. Even in the so-called "dry seasons" it is warm and wet. There is little change in the length of days and nights. Plants have plenty of light as well as moisture to help them grow all year.

The trees are evergreen but their leaves are broad, not narrow like the evergreen trees of the coniferous forest. The trees grow to great

Courtesy of the AMERICAN MUSEUM OF NATURAL HISTORY

heights to get as much sunlight as possible. At different times of the year they lose their leaves for short periods, but the forest is never bare as the deciduous forest is in winter. They put forth flowers and fruits at different times which means the birds and animals which feed only on nectar and fruits of the trees can always find food. There is no need for them to leave this biome to seek food, and birds that spend the summer in the deciduous forest spend the winter here.

Trees of this biome form the forest into a series of layers. It is their adaptation to the climate. The tops of the tallest evergreens form an almost continuous awning over two or more lower layers formed by the crowns of lower trees. Beneath all of this are several layers of woody shrubs. These layers divide the bird and animal life of the forest.

Great woody vines climb the trees, and plants which grow high overhead send down aerial roots right through the trees in search of food. Palm trees, mangrove trees and tree orchids are found here. Of the animals, probably the best known are the brightly colored birds which include the reddish egret, roseate spoonbill and heron.

In the tropical forest of South America is an animal found nowhere else on earth—the well known sloth. A primitive animal, he is able to hang upside down from branches while he eats and sleeps.

Man was probably a tropical animal originally. Today, however, he finds this biome to be an uncomfortable one. When he must live in this hot and wet biome, he tries to make the temperature more comfortable and the air dryer.

CHAPARRAL AND WOODLAND

These two biomes are grouped together because they represent such a small area of the earth. They are dense forest-like growths of stunted trees or hard-leaved shrubs. Usually they are found on mountain slopes in warm and dry parts of the world. In Europe, they appear about the Mediterranean Sea. Chaparrals may also be found in the southwestern part of the United States. The thick growth and the interweaving of the roots of these stunted trees are valuable because they help keep water in the soil and soil in place on the mountain slope.

Some birds and animals wander into this biome to gather food, but they seldom make it their homes.

Courtesy of the AMERICAN MUSEUM OF NATURAL HISTORY

SAVANNA BIOME

This grassland is different from the grasslands biome because it receives enough rainfall to allow some trees or shrubs to grow. Usually the trees or shrubs grow together in clumps. This biome is usually found in the warm parts of the world where heavy rainfall is followed by a long dry time. In order to continue life, the trees and grasses have to adapt to this condition of drought.

In the Savanna of Africa, zebra, hartebeests and giraffe live. In the Savanna of Australia live the replacement species of kangaroo and emu.

Courtesy of the AMERICAN MUSEUM OF NATURAL HISTORY

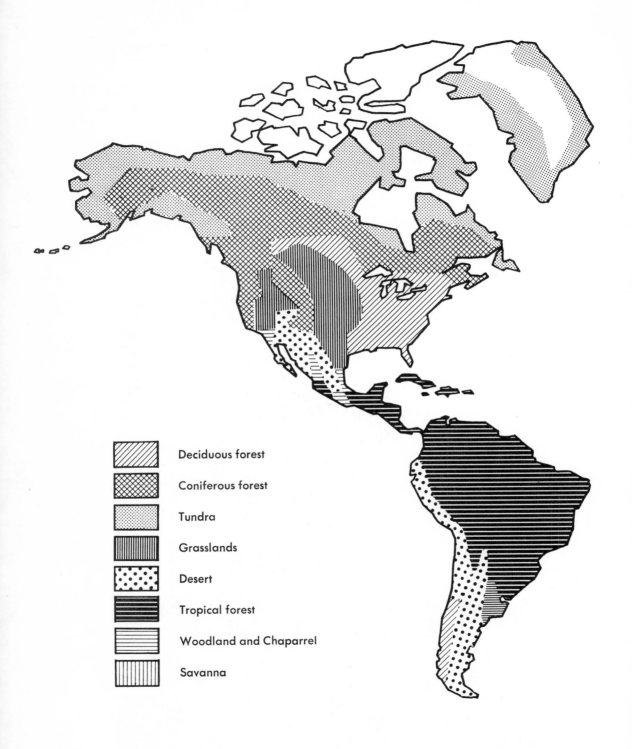

Deciduous forest

Coniferous forest

Tundra

Grasslands

Desert

Tropical forest

Woodland and Chaparrel

Savanna

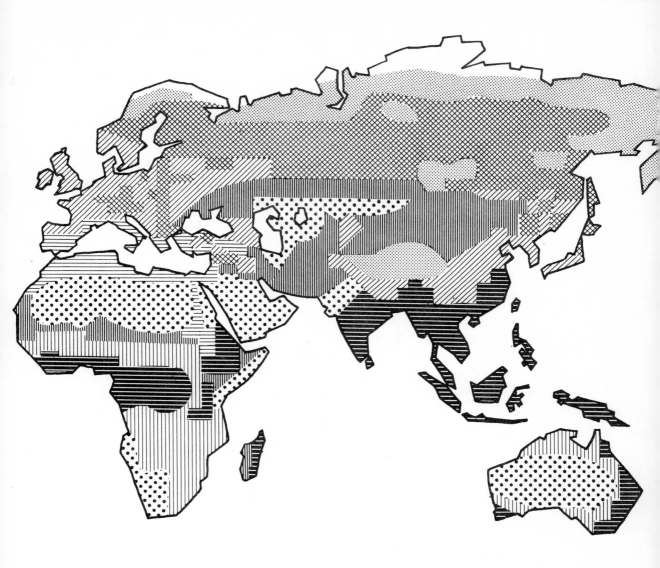

This map shows the nine generally recognized land biomes of the world as they would be if man did not interfere with them. The two smaller areas are grouped together. The biomes run across the surface of the earth in latitudinal zones parallel to the equator because environment is formed by *climate*—the average of weather conditions over a long period of time in each geographical area, as determined by air pressure, heat, wind and moisture.

Heat energy from the sun reaches the successive biomes and changes the temperature. The biomes follow in like order from the equator to the poles—tropical forest changes to deciduous forest, then gives way to the coniferous forest and finally to tundra.

Do you know in which biome you live? How do you know? Are you able to observe the trees, plants, birds and animals that make their natural home there? Are there great changes in the temperature and the length of day and night in winter and summer?

Have you ever lived in or visited another biome? When you go on a vacation seeking a warmer summer climate during the winter, are you doing as the birds do when they go south? If you do visit another biome in winter or summer, you may notice many changes in climate, length of the day and kinds of birds, plants, and animals.

There is another way in which you can observe the changes which climate makes in a biome—simply by climbing a high mountain. If you started to climb a high mountain in the tropics, you would find that at its foot is a hot tropical forest. As you climbed, you would reach a cooler deciduous forest. Climbing higher, you would find a still cooler coniferous forest which would end at the "timber line" where only a few twisted trees grow. As these disappeared, you would find rocks covered with lichen and mosses. If the mountain were high enough, you would find snow and ice near the summit as you do in the tundra.

This is the way the changing biomes might show on a mountain which rises out of a tropical forest. No biomes would end or begin abruptly. There would be a gradual change from one biome to another. For example, the trees of the coniferous forest would grow further and further apart. Gradually they would give way to the twisted dwarfed trees of the timberline. The biomes start lower on the northern side of the mountain. Less light and heat reach that side and as a result the temperature is lower and less plant growth takes place. ⟶

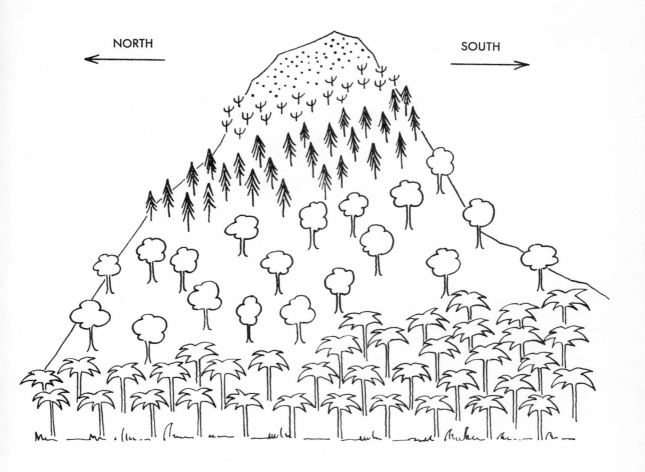

NORTH ← 　　　　　SOUTH →

TUNDRA

TIMBER LINE

CONIFEROUS FOREST

DECIDUOUS FOREST

TROPICAL FOREST

Chapter 7

COMMUNITIES

In reading about the different biomes of the world you have had a quick look at some of the plants and animals which may be found in each. You found that forests develop only where there is enough rain for the trees to make sufficient food from the sun and soil to support life. Where there was not enough rain or sunlight, plants made special changes in their structure in order to live. The same thing is true of animals. They have to change their eating and nesting habits and sometimes their body structures to fit their surroundings. This process of making adjustments to the environment is called *adaptation* (ad-ap-tay-shon).

You can see examples of adaptation all about you. If you live in a city or a suburban area, you will know that some plants and animals have adapted to the environment created by man. Dogs and cats have learned to live in man's cities. Over many centuries man, too, has adapted to the city environment. In order to survive in the crowded city, man has had to develop control of his emotions and increase his mental powers. He has adapted so that he can meet the needs of life in a crowded city culture. Physically man has adapted too. He has developed resistance to diseases such as small-pox and tuberculosis which spread rapidly in crowded city conditions.

If you should explore any biome, you would soon discover many small parts in which plants and animals are quite different from those described as living in the main part of the biome.

If you live in the deciduous forest biome, you know from your own experience that it is not completely covered with trees which lose their leaves in autumn. There are parts where man has changed the natural environment so much that it can hardly be recognized. If you go to a city park, you will find open grassy areas, asphalt paths, flower beds, shrubs, trees and perhaps a pond. You may even find trees which are not native to the biome, trees which man has brought in because he likes them. In the country, you will not find continuous forest either. Besides the woodland areas, you will find large and small roads, meadows, hedgerows, and miles of strips clear of trees where gas pipe lines or high tension electric wires run. There will also be swamps, rivers, small streams, lakes and ponds.

These different places are known as communities. Ecologists consider a *biotic community* to be any collection of plants and animals living in a given area which are held together by their relationship with, and dependence upon, each other.

Here ecologists can study how each community is organized and how each part affects all of the other parts. An ornithologist may study *one* bird in a community, a biologist *one* plant, an entomologist *one* insect, and a zoologist *one* animal. The ecologist must study all of them so that he can understand their relationship to each other and to their environment.

In a city park you would find certain plants, birds, insects, worms and small animals that make homes in the open grassy areas. This is one community. The lake in the park is another community because here another group of plants, animals, birds and insects carry on their lives.

The countryside offers many communities each with its own plant and animal population. The roadside, the meadow, the hedgerow, the swamp or even a fallen tree may be a biotic community.

The borderline where two different communities meet and blend is known as an *ecotone* (ek-o-tone). It may be where the forest and grassland meet, where the sea meets the shore, or the bank of a lake or stream in a city park. An ecotone is a busy place and exciting to explore, for where two communities meet, you will find a greater variety of plant and animal life. In search of food, the birds and animals of each community venture into the open where you can see them more easily.

If you have a garden, you can create an ecotone by providing trees, shrubs, open lawns, flowers and bird baths, houses and feeders. Your ecotone may attract migrating birds that would not usually visit a wide open space with few trees or shrubs and no water.

A careful observation of a community shows that plants and animals live together in agreement. Every living thing has a will for life to go on. People have the mistaken idea that animals in a natural community are enemies. People believe that *predators* (pred-a-tors) (animals which prey on other animals) are waiting—ready to snatch every passer-by. *Ethology* (e-thol-o-je), the study of an animal's normal behavior, shows that this is not true. Both plants and animals appear to avoid direct competition with others if it might injure or kill them. Only when a community becomes overcrowded or is upset does competition for food increase and bring danger.

Because of the great "will to live," all living things seem to "cooperate" as well as "compete" with each other. When life is carried on normally in a community, the members live peacefully together. Often one will alert another to a common danger. You can observe this in a city park or street or in a suburban garden where pigeons, sparrows, starlings and other birds live together. There may be some "pecking" at the smaller birds who come to feed, but it is not a fight to the death. Watch chipmunks or squirrels feeding and chasing, and you will soon realize that much of the chasing seems to be in fun. If a real fight should develop, the other animals in the area show great concern even though they are not involved.

The predator is an important and necessary part of any community,

52

for he helps to keep the population in balance. Predators seek food with great skill and kill their prey quickly. They kill because they are hungry and must have food to continue life. They do not kill because they hate the prey. They probably have no more feeling for the prey than you do for the steer from which your hamburger came.

Like every other part of the biosphere, a community is changing constantly. There are the obvious changes of night and day, winter and summer. These are known as *cyclic* (sik-lic) *changes*—changes which occur over and over.

Some other changes in a community take place over a much longer period—changes made by the ice ages long ago, changes made in the geological ages when great masses of land were lifted high and great new mountain ranges formed.

Plants and animals slowly change too. They adapt to the changes in their communities. Ecologists have found in studying communities that they can tell in advance what changes will occur. *Ecological succession* is the process of orderly change which occurs in communities of plants and animals. What happens as this succession takes place in an open meadow made by man as he cleared the land to grow grain? Fire, started in the forest by lightning, may have cleared a large space. If the meadow is left to nature, a certain succession of events will take place. In the deciduous forest biome, the root stocks of grass and flowers will grow. The wind will carry some seeds of annual wildflowers which will put out roots and grow. Grasshoppers, butterflies, meadowmice and meadowlarks will be among the members of the meadow community. They find an open meadow a good place to live.

If the grass is not mowed for several years, plant succession will continue and the meadow will gradually change. The wind will carry seeds of willow, maple and elm trees. These will put down roots and start growing, giving birds something to perch upon. The birds will carry in wild cherries and berries and, having eaten the fruit, will leave the seeds. Some of these seeds will grow, and a thicket will develop. Slowly the grasses will disappear because they cannot get enough sun and moisture. Squirrels, rabbits and other small animals who live in a thicket will come, and the community membership will change.

The squirrel will bring other seeds—beech, acorn and hickory nuts. Some will not be eaten but will put out roots and grow. As they develop, they will replace the thicket which cannot live in the shade of trees. Then the members of the community will change again. Owls, jays, chickadees and woodpeckers will take the place of meadow-larks and sparrows. Meadow-mice leave and racoon, porcupine and squirrel as well as other forest animals succeed them.

Changes continue, for there are trees which cannot live in the dense shady forest without sun. Slowly the willow and birch disappear. The sugar maple and beech tree are adapted to the dense forest conditions and are able to carry on life. They will replace themselves as they grow old and die. No other tree will force them out, and this forest community will go on for years with the plants, birds and animals living in balance. This is called a *climax community,* the final group of plants and animals which go on reproducing themselves instead of having another kind take their place. This takes many years, more than your whole lifetime, so that you may see only a part of the succession. This orderly succession of plant life is the way in which the various biomes were formed.

Perhaps you would enjoy observing a community near where you live. A rotting log in a park or woodland is an interesting one. Here again you will probably see only part of the succession of the community as the log is slowly returned to soil.

If you find a rotting log in a park or woodland you may find the answers to the following questions.

Can you see where the tree stood when it was alive? Is the bark still on the tree? Can you lift it off? Is anything underneath the

54

bark? Is there any fungus on the tree? Do you find the wood hard when you poke it with your ruler? Do you see any holes bored in the wood? Can you tell by their size who might have made them? Is the log hollow? Is anything living there? Lift the log. Do you find insects, spiders, lizards or salamanders underneath? Put the log back so that you do not disturb the community. Where the log meets the ground can you tell where the log ends and the soil begins? Poke this part of the log with your ruler. Does it flake and look like soil? Are there any young plants or trees finding a root hold on the old log?

ECOLOGICAL SUCCESSION OF A DEAD TREE

During its long lifetime the tree used materials from its environment—soil, water and sunlight. It has slowly died but still remains standing in the forest. In the ecological succession which follows the tree will provide changing habitats and therefore changing communities of animals, insects and plants will find a place to live. While living within and on the wood they will help the tree disintegrate. By decay the wood will turn into *humus* which is the organic part of the soil. Humus mixes with the soil and returns food to the soil.

Animals climbing the tree as well as wind, snow and ice help break off the small top branches. The bark becomes loose and beetles burrow under the bark to feed on the inner layer of bark and others on the outer wood of the trunk. Reproductive spores of fungi enter the small open places and start gathering food from the damp wood. The woody shelf fungi and small mushrooms are the reproductive parts of these plants and a sign of the breaking down of wood which is going on under the bark.

These living organisms are not here by accident. They are the animals and plants which can best survive under the conditions in the tree at the present time.

This rectangular hole was made in the dead tree by a pileated woodpecker when he came to feed on insects. Boring into the bark he might find carpenter ants, beetles, termites, insect larvae, and other insects which attract him and other woodpeckers and nuthatches.

Holes in the tree serve as homes for birds and other animals such as racoons and squirrels. The activities of all these insects, animals and fungi help break down the tree. Finally, it falls to the forest floor.

This fall changes the location of the dead tree community. The membership changes because the conditions have changed. Birds and squirrels leave to find new homes. The ground is damp and this causes fungi to increase their growth as they reach out to feed on new parts of the log.

Beetles, centipedes, slugs and earthworms go on breaking down the wood. The earth worms eat and digest the organic matter and mix it with the soil beneath the log. Salamanders find the moist underside of the log a good place to live. In dry parts of the fallen tree spiders may live.

Chipmunks may hide in the hollow parts of the fallen tree. With squirrels they may sit on top of the log feeding because here they are able to watch for danger. They may leave behind a beechnut or acorn which may put out roots in the moss which has started to grow on the log.

Time goes by and the fallen log collapses as the wood rots. Animal homes are destroyed, wood-borers must leave as their food supply is gone. In the thick moss which has grown new plants appear such as ferns and Canada May-flower, taking the place of the fungi. The community changes and it becomes hard to tell where the wood leaves off and the soil begins.

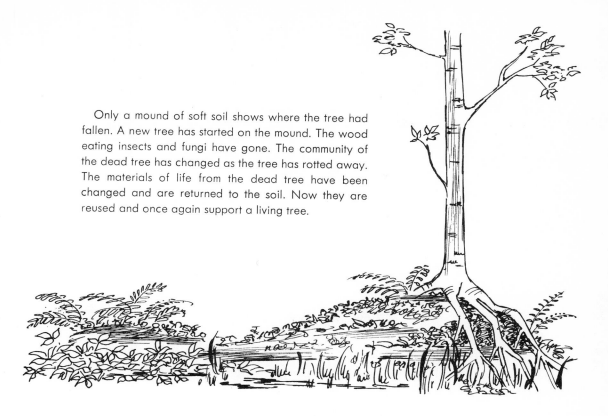

Only a mound of soft soil shows where the tree had fallen. A new tree has started on the mound. The wood eating insects and fungi have gone. The community of the dead tree has changed as the tree has rotted away. The materials of life from the dead tree have been changed and are returned to the soil. Now they are reused and once again support a living tree.

Another good way to observe ecological succession is to start with a bare spot. If you have a garden, dig up all the plants in one small area of about a square foot. Record, when you do this digging, the number, size and types of insects, worms and animals you find. Record the kinds of plants you find. For a year set aside a special time when you record all that you find happening at the digging. Compare the reports as you go along.

If you live in the city, you might fill a box with soil and place it on your fire escape or terrace, making sure it is secure and that the wind will not blow it over. Keep a record of what happens to this soil. Does it blow away? When and why? Do any plants start to grow? Do any insects or worms appear? Where do they come from? Will they be able to live in the box of soil?

Chapter 8

HABITAT AND NICHE

If you want to learn more about a certain animal, bird or plant, the first thing you have to know is where to find it. You would not look for a cactus in the far north or a polar bear in the tropics! Where a plant or animal lives, finds food and shelter and raises its young is its *habitat* (hab-i-tat). Many kinds of plants and animals share the same habitat.

When you know where the animal or plant you are interested in lives, then you will want to know more about its place in the community. What does it give to the community? What does it take from it? How is it affected by its environment, and how does it in turn affect the environment?

If you watch one special plant or animal carefully, you may find where it prefers to make its home, gather food, sun itself, rest, get water. You will also learn who are its "friends and enemies." Taken all together, these form the special place in the community which an ecologist calls a *niche* (nitch). The niche of an organism depends on what it does as well as where it lives. *Your* niche is made up of your home and family, the school you attend and what you do after school. If you are a boy with a newspaper route, you affect many people. Without you, many people would not know what was happening in the community. You affect them if you are late in delivering the paper; they probably get cross. A girl who baby-sits affects the community also. Without her, mothers could not shop or go out in the evening.

Ecologists have found that no two species of plant or animal can occupy the same niche at the same time. While they are in flight the dragonfly, swift and bat all feed on insects. The dragonfly feeds mostly at dusk over the edges of streams and ponds. The swift feeds all day while the bat catches his share of insects at night. All three occupy similar niches yet they do not directly compete with each other. Study shows there are smaller niches among similar animals and insects. Smaller species of dragonflies may be seen feeding closer to the water than larger ones. The use animals and plants make of time and space to fill different niches in their habitat is fascinating.

Anyone who has ever watched a daisy knows that it is a flower whose blossoms open early in the day and close at evening. Such flowers provide food for bees and other insects.

Other plants, such as the four o'clock, open late in the day or at night. Moths find them a good place to find food. When plants and insects work together in this way, both gain as they provide more niches.

The difference in the use of space to make niches can be seen by watching the animals or plants of any habitat. Birds, such as the sparrow, feed on the ground but nest in shrubs and vines. Other birds, like the woodpecker, take insects from the bark of a tree for food. Usually they nest in a hole in a tree. Difference in place of feeding and nesting helps reduce the competition for the necessities of life.

61

The developing and keeping of niches explains many happenings in the world of nature. An insect that inhabits a strange and difficult niche in most homes is the clothes moth. His ancestors probably lived on the larva of mites and ticks. In order to fill the special niche he now occupies, he underwent great physical changes and was forced to change his diet. There are few other animals able to digest the fibrous protein found in wool, hair and leather. The moth larvae live on or in the fabric and have no apparent supply of water. As a result, they can now absorb water from damp air. A dry house is a threat to their lives.

The clothes moth can vary the length of its life as a larva. When food or water is hard to find, the larva rests or slows down its growth. It then develops into a small adult insect, as much as one-tenth the normal size. However, it still lives and reproduces.

This interesting insect has affected man in more ways than eating his woolen clothing. Dr. Paul H. Müller, a Swiss chemist, might never have discovered D. D. T. if the moth had not stubbornly adapted to its strange niche. In seeking a pesticide to kill them, Dr. Müller discovered D. D. T. which is also used to kill typhus lice, plague flies and malaria mosquitoes. Man has slowed down the spread of disease by the use of D. D. T. and, as a result, saved the lives of millions of people. The stubborn little clothes moth can be thought of as helpful to mankind because he helped lead to the discovery of D. D. T.

Scientists have many things to learn about niches. Some animals and insects do not stay in one niche all of their lives. The mosquito is one of these. He starts his life in still water. When he buzzes about our heads as we try to sleep on a hot summer night, we know he has left that niche!

Scientists know that to live each plant and animal must have its own niche. However, niches may overlap. Plants and animals invade each other's feeding and nesting places. How much and how far they may invade before one species pushes the other out is a complicated study. If a niche should become empty because an animal becomes extinct, it will be filled due to slow changes in another animal's feeding habits as the animal slowly reaches out to make use of the unused food supply. Changing and emptying of niches is an important part of the balance of nature. It is part of the process of ecological succession.

Man has often emptied a niche without thinking of the results. The porcupine was never a nuisance to early settlers of North America. A weasel-like animal called a fisher could swim under the porcupine, avoiding his dangerous quills and capturing him. The fisher kept the porcupine population in balance. Unfortunately, the fisher had a fine fur coat which man wanted. As a result, the fisher has been over-trapped in some parts of the country. In places where the fisher is no longer found, the porcupine population grows because no natural enemy keeps it in check. The porcupine now chews his way through valuable forest lands. If the niche of the fisher had not been disturbed, the porcupine would still have a natural enemy to keep the balance.

Man as an animal also has a niche. Man would leave his niche empty if he destroyed all of his kind in a nuclear war. What would happen then? Ecologists believe that not all life would be destroyed. As time went on, the deadly radiation would slowly die away. The evolution of other forms of life would continue and niches would be filled. However, ecologists believe that man would not evolve again to fill the niche he now does because the forms of life from which he developed no longer exist. The conditions which helped man to develop are no longer present.

Man secured and holds his present niche because of several remarkable adaptations. He has developed strong hands with straight agile fingers and thumbs which make it possible for him to grip, pick-up and carry things. Together with this, man developed the ability of hand and eye to work together. Other animals are able to grasp with forepaws and have developed good cooperation between paw and eye. Think of the monkey or ape. Squirrels and birds too use their feet as "hands," holding food or picking up material for nests. Dogs sometimes use a forepaw to hold a dish in place when eating. If man should leave his niche empty because of nuclear war, one of these other forms of life might survive, evolve and fill his niche.

Chapter 9

ENERGY

It is necessary in ecology to study and understand how the non-living part of the environment affects the living part. It is something amateurs can enjoy observing and understanding. Since all energy comes from the sun, without the sun there would be no life. The energy which comes from the sun may be changed from one kind of energy into another, but it is never created or destroyed.

The sun, a great sphere of hot gasses, is the center of our solar system. The distance between the sun and earth varies between 94,500,000 and 91,500,000 miles.

Light energy is given off by the sun and travels through space until it meets the earth's surface where it may change into heat energy. As the surface of the earth warms, so does the air close to it. The light and heat energy from the sun put into motion the machinery that makes conditions right for life on earth.

Without the light and heat, plants and animals could not live. The amount of heat and light received in different parts of the earth varies all the time and makes a difference in the way of life of all things. You will remember how each of the world's biomes is affected by differences in the lengths of days and seasons.

During a year's orbit around the sun, the earth is spinning, something like a top on its tilted axis. It takes a day for the earth to spin around once. The part of the earth facing the sun has daylight. When it is away from the sun, it is night. The exchange of light for dark affects all things. How does it affect you? A pet bird will go to roost when the sun goes down. However, a pet hamster is most active at night. Other animals, such as deer, are most active at dawn and dusk when the light intensity is low. They may also be quite active on dark, cloudy days and on moonlit nights.

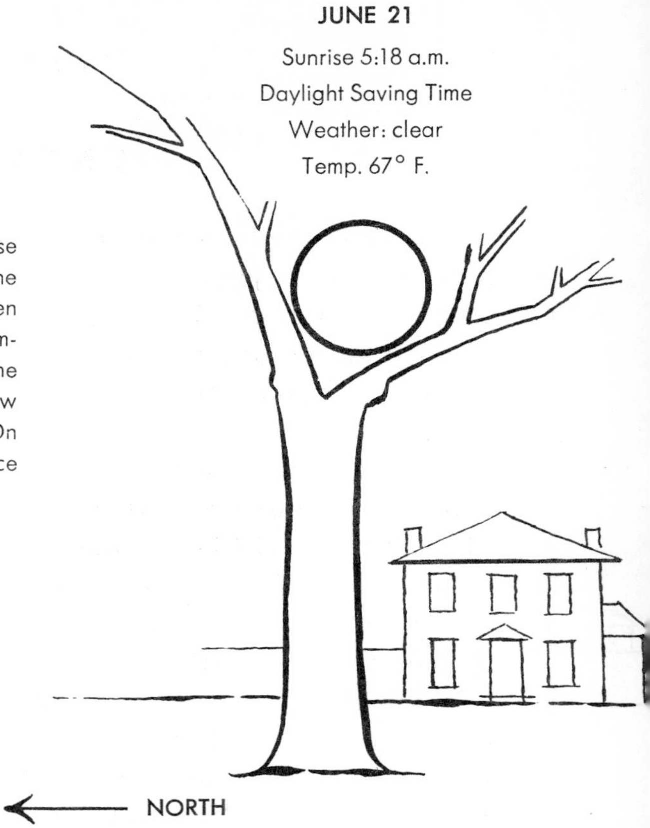

Sunrise 5:18 a.m.
Daylight Saving Time
Weather: clear
Temp. 67° F.

Looking out of an east window your sunrise mural might show something like this. On June 21 the sun may be seen rising through the green leaves of a large tree to the north. On September 21 it makes its appearance above the church steeple. December 21 it comes into view just over the chimney of a nearby house. On March 21 it appears above the steeple once more.

← NORTH

Changing seasons are caused by the tilt of the earth's axis. The warm concentrated rays of the sun reach the Northern Hemisphere from March to September when it is tilted toward the sun. These rays generate more heat than the less concentrated ones which spread as they reach the Northern Hemisphere from October to March. Days are longer and warmer from March to September, shorter and cooler from October to March. As the hours of daylight grow fewer and the nights longer, the temperature usually drops.

It is interesting to observe the position of the sun in the sky. Keep

SEPT. 21

Sunrise 6:42 a.m.

Daylight Saving Time

Weather: rain

Temp. 63° F.

MARCH 21

Sunrise 5:58 a.m.

Eastern Standard Time

Weather: rain

Temp. 40° F.

DEC. 21

Sunrise 7:17 a.m.

Eastern Standard Time

Weather: clear

Temp. 32° F.

SOUTH ⟶

a sunset, or (if you are an early bird) a sunrise mural record. From a place where you can see the sunrise or sunset, make a simple sketch of the horizon on a long piece of shelf paper. On the bottom, mark it to show which direction is north and which south. Start this record on either June 21 or December 21 when the sun will be farthest north or south. Make your observation once a month, marking on the mural where the sun rises or sets. To add interest, keep a record of the time and temperature also. The sun's journey across the sky will be apparent at the end of six months.

67

You will also see how the length of day and the temperature have changed. In truth, this is a record of something that does not happen. The sun does not rise or set. It is the way the earth keeps turning on its axis which makes it seem as if the sun is rising and setting.

The rays of the sun reach the earth in different concentrations all day as well as all year. The morning and evening rays are more spread out than at noon when they are more concentrated. That is why the temperature usually starts to climb near noon. You can observe this by watching the changing length of shadows during the day.

You can observe the different angles at which the light of the sun hits the earth at different times of the day. Choose a tree or a building which stands by itself and whose shadow you can easily see. Make a record of where the shadow edges are at sunrise, noon and in the evening. Do this once a month and record the changes.

These observations of the sun will show you only a small part of what happens when the light of the sun reaches the earth.

Chapter 10

FOOD CHAINS

It is interesting to trace the movement of the sun's energy as it travels through an ecosystem and the whole biosphere. The transfer of energy through an ecosystem by the producers (food makers), the consumers and the decomposers is called a *food chain*. Only green plants exposed to sunlight are able to make food filled with the sun's energy. These green plants are the first link in the food chain.

When an animal, a herbivore, eats a green plant, some of the energy of the sun will be passed along to the animal. This will be used for growth and for the energy needed to live and move about. The animal is the second link in the food chain.

When a second animal, a carnivore, eats the first animal, another transfer of energy is made, and another link is added to the food chain. This all sounds very simple, and it would be if all food chains were of the same length. Cow's milk comes from a short and simple chain with only two links. Grass on which a cow feeds is filled with energy from the sun. The cow in turn produces the liquid food or milk we drink. The grass-to-milk chain is a simple one. Most chains are more complicated because most animals eat a variety of foods. A fox may feed on several different foods and take some of the sun's energy from each. On the following page is a diagram of the simple food chain of a fox.

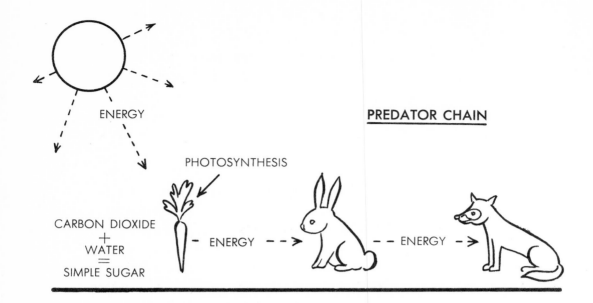

ENERGY

PREDATOR CHAIN

PHOTOSYNTHESIS

CARBON DIOXIDE
+
WATER
=
SIMPLE SUGAR

− − ENERGY − − → − − ENERGY − − →

PARASITE CHAIN

RASPBERRIES

SOIL NUTRIENTS
WATER

− − − ENERGY − − →

ENERGY − − →

SAPROPHYTE CHAIN

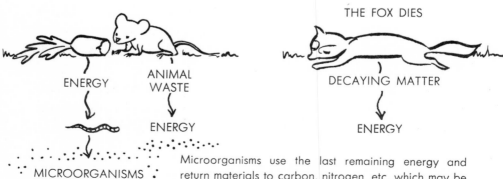

THE FOX DIES

ENERGY   ANIMAL
WASTE

DECAYING MATTER

ENERGY

ENERGY

MICROORGANISMS

Microorganisms use the last remaining energy and
return materials to carbon, nitrogen, etc. which may be
used again by green plants in an endless cycle.

Each time this eating process takes place, only a small part of the energy of the sun is passed along to the next consumer. Some energy is always lost to the consumer. This means that each consumer receives less of the energy from the sun than whoever ate before him. Thus, only a restricted number of "top" consumers, such as man, can be supported.

Scientists have divided food chains into three groups. The first which you have read about is the *predator chain* in which energy is transferred from the plant to the plant-eater and on to the carnivore, the flesh eater, who receives energy from the sun third-hand.

The parasite chain occurs when energy goes from a larger animal to a smaller one. A *parasite* is a plant or animal which attaches itself to another living thing called its "host." The parasite finds shelter and food. This relationship requires a delicate balance. If the parasite is too greedy, he may kill the host and in doing so destroy his niche. A bird taking a dust bath and preening himself is getting rid of parasites which live on his feathers and skin. Birds are known to be "hosts" to as many as twenty parasites from the time they hatch.

Plants too may be parasites and use another plant as "host." The seedling of dodder starts to grow like any ordinary plant. However, when it touches a green plant the dodder puts out rootlike projections into the green plant. The real root of the dodder wastes away. Then rootless and leafless the yellow-orange plant twines around its host, absorbing the food it cannot make for itself.

In *the saprophyte* (sap-ro-fite) *chain,* the energy from the sun is transferred from dead plants and animals to microorganisms. This takes place mostly out of sight under the soil. A *saprophyte* is an organism which lives on dead or decaying matter. It is one of the valuable decomposers of the ecosystem.

In the shady summer woods grow clumps of waxy-white Indian pipes. They are also called corpse plants. Perhaps the name comes from their ghostlike appearance or because they take nourishment from dead wood and leaves.

Even city dwellers may see saprophytes at work as a mushroom growing on dead wood or a shelf fungi on a dead branch. People consume the sun's energy through the saprophyte chain when they enjoy mushrooms.

There are two other ways that plants or animals live together. In *mutualism* (mew-tew-alizm) each member benefits from this way of life. In fact, one member cannot live without the other under natural conditions.

On rocks you often find a crust of grey-green substance called *lichen* (ly-ken). Lichen is algae and fungi living together. The thread of fungus supplies water to the green cells of algae which makes food for them both. The mutualism benefits each member.

Some animals also develop this kind of relationship. There is an interesting relationship between aphids and ants. Aphids are small parasitic insects which live on plants. Ants will care for aphids in the ant nest in early spring and later move them to a good feeding place on the stems or roots of plants. When an ant strokes an aphid, the aphid gives off a drop of clear sweet fluid. The ant drinks it just as man drinks cow's milk.

The second way in which plants or animals live together is called *commensalism* (kom-men-sa-lizm). It is a lopsided arrangement because only one member receives benefits. However, the other member is not hurt by this.

Near a flock of grazing sheep you will notice starlings. The birds feed on the living lice and ticks they gather from the sheep's wool.

The ocean is a good place to observe commensalism. Nearly every sponge, shellfish and worm burrow has another animal living on it. The "Spanish moss" which drapes itself on trees in the Southern and Western parts of the United States is one of the best known commensal plants.

Scientists describe both mutualism and commensalism with the term *symbiosis* (sim-be-oh-sis). It means the union of two living things that depend on each other for life.

Symbiosis may be a newly recognized evolutionary step in our environment, and the meaning and number of instances of symbiosis of algae loom very important.

Even though food chains may be separated from the environment for study and understanding, they are all interwoven, never-ending processes. They illustrate how all parts of the world of nature are dependent one on the other. Man studies the chains with growing interest and concern because half of the world's people go to bed hungry each night. There simply is not enough food for all. Man realizes that the earth's population is increasing rapidly. Unless he can produce more food, even more people will go hungry.

The knowledge of food chains has taught man that shorter food chains enable more people to survive in a given land area. The people of the Orient have always faced the problem of a too large population in a too small land area. They rely on a short food chain, eating rice instead of meat. They eat small fish instead of larger ones because less of the sun's energy is lost in transferring it from one fish to another. As the whole earth becomes more crowded, it will be even more crucial for man to use the knowledge of the transfer of energy through food chains, or people will starve.

Chapter 11

BIOGEOCHEMICAL CYCLES

Ecologists have made up a term to describe the travels of non-living substances they find moving through the environment. The term is biogeochemical cycle. It comes from "bio" which means life, and "geo" which means earth or soil, and "chemical" which refers to the elements which are the basic building blocks of nature. Some of the chemicals are carbon, nitrogen, phosphorus and oxygen which must always be available if life is to continue.

A "cycle" is a series of events or happenings that keeps repeating, like the turning of a bicycle wheel. *Biogeochemical cycle,* then, describes the way in which chemicals move unseen from the non-living environment to living things and then back again.

The cycle of nitrogen is essential to all living things. Nitrogen is an important part of all proteins and amino acids in living cells. Green plants must have it ready for use at all times if they are to grow. The amount ready for use regulates the flow of life. Nitrogen in the form of gas makes up almost eighty per cent of the earth's atmosphere. However, only a few plants and no animals can make use of nitrogen when it is in the form of gas. Nitrogen of the atmosphere must first be made usable to life by the nitrogen-fixing bacteria and algae of the soil. So tiny you would need a microscope to see them, they must capture free nitrogen to live. In doing this, they mix and change it into nitrogen salts, called nitrates.

When the bacteria die, the nitrates are released into the soil. Water then dissolves the nitrates and the plants are able to absorb them through their roots and grow. Once the plants have used the nitrogen in their growth, it passes through other living things by way of food chains.

The nitrogen returns from the living world to the soil when

THE NITROGEN CYCLE

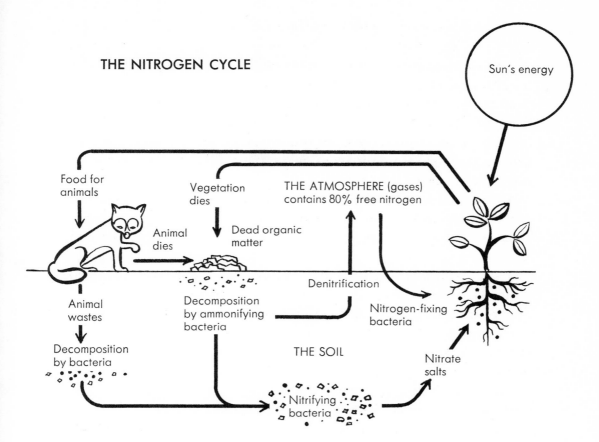

Sun's energy

Food for animals

Vegetation dies

THE ATMOSPHERE (gases) contains 80% free nitrogen

Animal dies

Dead organic matter

Animal wastes

Decomposition by ammonifying bacteria

Denitrification

Nitrogen-fixing bacteria

Decomposition by bacteria

THE SOIL

Nitrate salts

Nitrifying bacteria

animals excrete waste products or die. The decomposers break down these materials releasing the nitrogen as ammonia. At this part of the cycle, nitrifying bacteria use the ammonia and change it first to nitrites and then to nitrates which again make it available to plants through their roots.

In this cycle nitrogen is also returned to the atmosphere by denitrifying bacteria. Then the nitrogen is free, right back where it started from and ready to be re-used by the nitrogen fixing bacteria and algae of the soil.

An interesting plant family called legumes demonstrates the nitrogen cycle. Peas, clover, alfalfa, soy beans and lupine are examples. As the roots of these plants develop, a discharge from them forms small lumps of bacteria. The bacteria put out a discharge which deforms the tiny root hairs. A lump called a nodule then forms on the root. In it nitrogen is stored. The plant and bacteria work together to fix the nitrogen. In this symbiotic relationship, the bacteria receive food from the plant, while the plant and the soil around it get the nitrogen they need.

Another cycle necessary for life is the mineral cycle. Potassium, phosphorus and calcium are some of the minerals which circulate from the non-living part of the environment to the living part and back again.

The phosphorus cycle is typical. The greatest supply of this mineral is stored in rocks and other deposits. The phosphorus is released slowly into the atmosphere due to the action of wind, rain and snow. If you touch a large rock, you will feel that the surface is rough. It may have a great crack in it. The atmosphere has been at work slowly breaking and wearing down the rock and thus releasing phosphorus. Wetting and drying, freezing and thawing, slow erosion by wind and water loosen material from the exposed part of the rock.

There are other rock breakers always at work on rocks and even the brick of your school or apartment house. They are the grey-green lichen which cling to the rock like a scabby crust. As they pull on the rock by swelling in wet weather and shrinking in dry weather, they loosen tiny particles. They also loosen granules of rock as they secrete acids which dissolve the cementing matter of the rock. Scrape a little lichen off a rock and rub it between your fingers to feel the gritty pieces of rock it has broken down.

Through your magnifying glass, look at the lichen on the rock. You may find reindeer "moss," a common lichen. It is grey-green and through your glass, you will see its finely divided branches. It forms large, tangled masses which are soft and rather rubbery when wet, crunchy when dry.

If the grey-green lichen has branches with red tips, you have found another lichen whose red tops give it the name, British Soldiers. If the lichen is funnel-shaped and tipped with green or pink, it is called pixie cups.

Some of the phosphorus released by weather or lichen reaches the soil where it may be used by plants. Large amounts, however, are washed out to sea and settle to the bottom. These "lost" deposits cannot be re-used quickly; their return from the sea is a long slow process. Some cycle back to land via sea-birds, and some in fish harvested by man.

In mining phosphate rocks, man has interfered with the cycle. Phosphates do not return quickly enough for re-use by plants. Because men believe the phosphorus cycle is too slow, they help complete the cycle by adding phosphates to the soil to increase plant production. If man did not do this, he might not produce enough food for the increasing population.

This knowledge of the value of phosphorus is not recent. When early farmers planted potatoes, they would place an oval stone, called a "manure" stone, over them. The farmer found it made the soil richer and the harvest better.

On New England farms, people often find mysterious piles of "manure" stones put there long ago when the field was cleared for planting. The piles remained several years before they were used for walls, and farmers records show that the land around them would sprout three times the crop of the rest of the field.

There are also calcium, carbon, oxygen and water cycles.

In exploring cycles, ecologists have found that elements and compounds not necessary to life also circulate—cycles of strontium, ruthenium and D. D. T., for example. These chemicals may be dangerous to man. Once they are started on a cycle, they may be impossible to stop. They need careful study if they are to benefit, not harm, mankind.

Man must study these cycles to understand the danger he may create when he interferes with the cycle of necessary elements. He can upset the delicate balance between living things and their environment. With understanding, he may be able to help keep the cycles in order. This is the chief purpose of conservationists. The study of ecology has changed the meaning of conservation. No longer is it simply the preservation and protection of natural resources. With this broader understanding of the giving and receiving between living things and their environment, man has come to think of conservation in terms of applying his knowledge of ecology to making wise choices about his environment and its resources.

Chapter 12

ECOLOGY AND YOU

Whether you make your home in the "inner city," an urban area or the country, this elementary exploration of ecology may help you to understand what is happening in the natural world in which you live. It may help you to realize the importance of protecting the natural environment so that nature can continue to renew natural resources.

Perhaps you will decide to become an ecologist. There is new and exciting work for ecologists to do in agriculture, forestry, land use, city planning and wild life management.

If you continue your interest in the out-of-doors, this exploration of ecology may help you to realize the importance and value of seeing that the balance of nature is kept. How can *you* do this? There are many ways. See to it that wild life is protected where you live. The wild creatures who share city and urban areas are important. They not only contribute beauty and pleasure, but also play an important part in setting up a balance. Sea gulls help keep rivers, harbors and beaches clean. Purple martins help reduce the number of mosquitoes; the sparrow hawk and owl catch rodents.

Trees, shrubs, grass, weeds and flowers are wildlife that add beauty to the world. They also help to keep the air cooler and more moist and reduce the amount of dust and dirt in the air.

By being aware of what will affect the environment of your community and nation, you can be ready to support laws for intelligent planning of cities and laws to keep the air and water free of pollution. You can support laws designed to set aside valuable open areas not only for recreation but also for "laboratories" where ecologists can study nature at work in an area unchanged by man.

Today, man's attempt to conquer outer space captures everyone's imagination. Of far greater importance, however, is man's quest to make proper use of the life-supporting natural resources of his everyday environment.

INDEX WITH REFERENCE GLOSSARY

INDEX WITH REFERENCE GLOSSARY

Numbers in **BOLD TYPE FACE** *indicate page where definition of term is given.*

ABOUT THE AUTHOR

Mrs. Billington has worked with children in many different areas. At present she is a Conservation Education Aide with the Mamaroneck Public Schools. She divides her time between her home in Larchmont, N. Y. and a log cabin in the Berkshire Mountains.

She is married and mother of a teen-age son.

Mrs. Billington is a member of the National Wildlife Federation, The Massachusetts and National Audubon Societies, and hopes her book will encourage more young people to participate in the work of such organizations.

ABOUT THE ARTIST

Mr. Galster has illustrated many books for children, especially in the science field. He has designed book jackets and record album covers and has painted murals for hotels in New York, Boston and Florida. Mr. Galster is also well known for his poster designs for the Broadway theatre.

Born in Dollville, Illinois, he grew up in Mansfield, Ohio, and served with the U.S. Army Engineers in Europe. He travels extensively, is a serious photographer and collects books and oriental sculpture. Mr. Galster lives in New York City.